Ocean Effects

poems

Ocean Effects

Brendan Galvin

Louisiana State University Press
Baton Rouge

NATIONAL
ENDOWMENT
FOR THE ARTS

This publication is supported in part by an award from the National Endowment for the Arts.

Published by Louisiana State University Press
Copyright © 2007 by Brendan Galvin
All rights reserved
Manufactured in the United States of America
First printing

Designer: Michelle A. Neustrom
Typeface: Rotis Serif
Printer and binder: Edwards Brothers, Inc.

Library of Congress Cataloging-in-Publication Data

Galvin, Brendan.
    Ocean effects : poems / Brendan Galvin.
        p. cm.
    ISBN 978-0-8071-3266-1 (alk. paper) — ISBN 978-0-8071-3267-8 (pbk. : alk. paper)
    I. Title
    PS3557.A44O25 2007
    811'.54—dc22

                                                                                2006037199

Grateful acknowledgment is made to the editors of the following publications, in which
the poems listed first appeared, sometimes under slightly different titles: *Atlantic Monthly,*
"A Mile Down the Road from Home" (2006), "The Mice" (2007); *Cortland Review* (online),
"Horse of Chernobyl, Horse of Lascaux" (2007); *Florida Review,* "Sgt. Newton and the Crows"
(2005); *Gettysburg Review,* "Doffing & Donning: An Exchange of Letters," "Letter from
George Ludlow, Merchant, to Roger Williams," "A Proposal of Banishment" (all 2004); *Hotel
Amerika,* "How Winter Left Town," "Sgt. Newton's Indie Film Debut" (both 2005); *Hudson
Review,* "Hard Evidence" (2007); *Image,* "Of Rivers, Theologies, and Persons Infamous" (2004),
"A Second Coming at Providence Plantation" (2007); *Laurel Review,* "Sgt. Crocker Newton on
the Usual Suspects" (2002); *Missouri Review,* "Mystery Squid" (2002), "Sgt. Newton Recollects
the Return of Thane Gould to Endicott, Massachusetts, in the Winter of 1977" (2003); *Notre
Dame Review,* "Moxie Hogan's Alibi" (2006); *Ploughshares,* "Oyster Money" (2006); *Sewanee
Review,* "Roger Williams's Shipwreck Letter to the Citizens of Providence Colony" (2007);
Shenandoah, "As in a Succession of Russian Dolls," "Letter of Roger Williams to John
Winthrop, Jr.," "The Snow Trial," "Splash" (all 2004), "Corps of Discovery," "Letter from Cold
Harbor" (both 2006); *Southern Review,* "Samuel Gorton: Letter of Roger Williams to William
Blackstone" (2004); "Forty Pines," "Ocean Effect," "Stations" (all 2005), "A Reliquary," "A
10th Century Pew End in the Faroes" (both 2006); *Swink* (online), "Roy Olafsen, Cape Cod
Craftsperson, Tells All" (2004); *Virginia Quarterly Review,* "Canoeing with Master Williams"
(2005), "The Labrador Summer" (2006).

In memory of Ned McLaughlin,
who showed us where home is.

Contents

I

Forty Pines

Now we are open one way to July,
one way to the winter Atlantic.
What parable of change will heal
these spaces? Necessity says
I should blame the turpentine beetles
who drilled some of these trunks until
their sap flowed into stiff ripples.
These woods—where Bob Morris, dead
twenty years, herded cows when he
was a boy and this was a field—
are old forest now, the oaks pushing
the pines out. Each was a singular
presence, leaning its own way, bulging
here and there as if for the hell of it,
and we rode out storms with them,
at times even swaying in empathy.
Still, I could claim it was wisdom
not to trust these seventy-footers
anymore, though I've spent more than
half my life walking their windfalls
of bronze needles where a lawn
would have been their betrayal.
But hadn't I cut one off the roof after
a nameless December blow? Didn't they
drop branches like serious wings
here and there in the dark? All these
fresh stumps frothing pitch, these limbs
like bone breaks, the sky over the ocean
deepening, and Andy climbing
with his rooster spurs into a green
crown he's rigging with cat's cradles,
holding consultations aloud with
himself between cigarettes,
his chainsaw dangling like a tail.
On snow-moon nights the owl won't
sing as close, and what will relay

the sound of surf to us with its branches?
No pollen to print our feet on the floors
in June, and no more bluejays
born with gray buzzcuts in a pine crotch
by our windows. Flurries of wrong snowflakes
drift down on this disaster. The reek of their going
is everywhere. Bring on the dwarf goddam
fruit trees, twigs in arty pots we can carry
into the house when the weather starts.

Splash

And I forgot the cardinal's
sanctuary lamp retreating deeper
into the trees, and ignored a blacksnake
sliding, head aloft, newly untangled
from hibernation,
assessing me as I passed.

When I got to the river
the surface was too hugely roiled
for a muskrat's dive or a shag's,
it was almost the "footprint"
a whale leaves when it sounds
for the depths, but that wasn't

what came up blowing water
like a kid after a dive,
its brown-golden head too big
for a weasel's, and rose up
to its shoulders seeing me there,
its tail working behind—

a river otter, a five-footer,
no goofy stuffed toy, but almost
smiling, the way a salamander
turned up under a log seems to smile
as if to say, *You have found me out.*

Though rumored all the way from
Pond Village to those freshwater reaches
where only the odd kayaker might go,
sometimes the thing seen once
in its right place
is spontaneous as a splash—

minutes, it must have been,
before its brown dissolve,
each in our way treading water,
supporting an end of our
sixty-foot stream of astonishment.

As in a Succession of Russian Dolls

A furry lump like the back of a brown creeper
on a side of the deck's newel post, then
the earlets, and one stick-leg flung out
as if in afterthought, its foot

clutching a splinter—bat, upside-down
bat—maybe just staggered out of
hibernation into the shock of cold,
and saturated with April rain,

risen before the insects that could fire
its blood. I left it to dry, but this afternoon
by the marsh, I caught

a pre-bird, post-butterfly dither
of indecision coming my way, the jittery
misdirections of bat flight,
like the heartbeat of a bad time,

as when the ingenue presses
the back of her hand to her lips and casts
a look of horror out into the audience.

But nothing's rabid here,
or so we've been assured, though now,
dangling head down from the yellow
traffic sign, its proxy sun, or else
hanging on until the first mosquito hatch,

it looked like origami gone all wrong,
and I went home and slipped a shovel under
bat number one, dropped it light as a leaf

onto the deck, a hollow pelt—only the suit
the second bat had climbed out of, perhaps,
as in a succession of Russian dolls, each
inside another, the husk of things to come.

The Labrador Summer
1833

Above latitude fifty, seasick,
as far north as he'd ever go,
Audubon understood why
they called it the land God gave
to Cain. Unable to sleep or stand,
he rocked in his bunk aboard
the schooner *Ripley,* as in
the higher branches of a tree,
considering how many ways
the word *Labrador* defined
a dismal coast, its unforgiving
stone pressing from cliffsides
kept raw by gales, a country
too tough even for sheep.
And the sea itself, tossing
and rolling stones, heaping
the shores with them, piling
them on each other like egg fields
dangerous to cross. He saw how
dirty weather could fool you,
lifting to reveal a fleet of sails
that in his glass turned
snowbanks, though it was June
and butterflies drifted above them
for the moss-kept flowers. Another
change of anchorage and it would feel
like Boston in December, save for
mosquitoes thick as those
in Plaquemines Parish bayous.
From a harbor without a name
he wrote, The bird for this place
must be the blackpoll warbler, its song
like the clicking of pebbles together
five or six times, apt for a land
with no earth, only stone,

and moss you sank through
to the knees or deeper, and evergreens
you tromped through like a giant
because they stood a foot tall.
On islands sprinkled across
endless bays, every fissure in rock
seemed to hold a cormorant
or guillemot tending its eggs.
He was forty-eight, weary
and often soaked with bog walking.
He'd counted nearly a hundred and fifty
schooners together on the cod banks,
smelled harbors fouled with fish waste,
looked everywhere for a pied duck,
its kind gone from the earth forty years later.
Drawing from first light at two A.M.
until the pencil cramped in his
hand, he cursed fog that dripped
from a spar onto the paper,
and the blackflies scribbling
at his face. Seventeen hours
at the table some days, not to compete
with the Creator, only to copy His works,
to finish the birds on his list,
to add some wild peas and a Labrador
tea-plant to his drawing of
a willow grouse.

Ocean Effect

This morning the harbor's surface looked oily,
as though a boat had gone down,
and I counted the draggers just to be sure,

The Holy Child, Curlew, Avaricious, Azore Rose
and the others, none missing, all waiting to be
locked into their moorings as the frazil ice began,

a suspension of frozen spicules that would thicken
into a soupy layer textured like grease.
In the bay window an amaryllis that usually
leaned on its long stem toward last evening's sunset—

as though to travel there, or to draw on whatever warmth
would maintain its four red-orange blossoms—had turned
back into the room, quailing from the weather.

Four below zero, too cold to snow as they say, but nobody
told that blur on clarity setting out across the water
a few miles off, then here, blowing in horizontally,
not settling, passing among the trees,

only an inch of it on the ground after four days
of ocean effect. The bay ice will build to shuga
in a matter of hours, spongy white, then to nilas
and pancake ice, floes, a field tented

like a Civil War encampment I could try to cross
from the wharf to the cove, risking myself
for mythic status. Wiser to stay by this amaryllis,

its January flowering aimed at the cardinal points,
looking as if any minute it might crackle into speech
and issue instructions for survival.

Mystery Squid

They say it lives miles down
in that wet obsidian
we crawled from, below
Martini's Law, down where
things, if they can, create
their own light.
            All we know
of its country is an accurate
reading of our own ignorance,
but in photographs that thing
looks like a blown-back
umbrella, handle and spokes,
fabric gone, until we
recall it's twenty feet long,

the size of a tree uprooted and
drifting sidewise where
pressure of depth
has exacted stringency
and its arms like ten sticky
branches trap prizes

yet to be named, blinks
and inklings, articulated wisps,
eclectic pulsings, a magpie
hoard where no magpie
can live, rhythms fleshed out,
tidbits on which this living
Giacometti thrives.

Where it moves with random
tail-lights toward memory's
submarine canyons, our loneliness
is as much without meaning

as silence, our disbelief is only
the self-saving doubt of a field hand
witnessing a space shot: "That thing
ain't going to no moon."

A 10th Century Pew End in the Faroes

After Surtsey's volcanic slopes, red and black
as those barrels of ash and clinkers I lugged
from coal cellars as a kid, I came to
the Vestmanna Islands, place of the West Men
or Irish, where I caught a promising hint of you
in Icelandic, old abbot: *I still live, and you will, too,*
arching above a graveyard gate.

Did my predilection for islands
come with the laying on of your name,
or from the insular self I learned early,
the one Brendan in a neighborhood of Tonys
and Sals, fighting for my name's strangeness
before it translated to a litany of ports and islands,
Celtic and Norse, alliterative, assonant?

After Kerry, Iona, then stony Mingulay, and Barra,
Benbecula, both Uists, North and South, and Kirkwall,
Lerwick's deepwater crossroads, and Muckle Flugga's
north-leaning shelves pointed a way to harbors
whose names end in "haven," villages tucked into fjords
off punishing seas, glaciers that curve down from
mountains and deliver the mist door to door.

From Mykines, that mountain of birds,
did you watch the northwest-going wedges of geese,
gray on gray, and ask, Why do they pass that way
unless across there is land? They know you in Kirkjubour,
Heimaey and Flatey as in Ardfert and Clonfert,
Brendan. All along that stepping-stone route
of sea caves and black shores I found you
in vestiges, the rubble of chapels you founded,

and here carved in wood in this pew end in Tórshavn
you're as burly as in any stained-glass window
in Galway, proof the oral tradition

has kept you true: no cress-and-springwater monk,
but a legend not as given to fasting
as you might have been, your face across centuries
teaching the difference between tourist and pilgrim.

Roy Olafsen, Cape Cod Craftsperson, Tells All

First time I look at their lot with the new clients
I give them my Thoreau Moment, just walking around
like I'm studying the situation, gazing off into the woods
down the back, even rolling the dirt between
my thumb and fingers. Then I step off the distance
in a trance from the trees to road's edge, and check
where the sun's at, as if I could improve on
its location with a few minor adjustments.

The ponytail's a badge of sensitivity. I tug on it
to show I'm thinking hard, make them wonder
was I at Woodstock. Americans are suckers for nostalgia.
All that time not a word leaves my mouth, even when
I go from several arbitrary places to the boundary sticks.
After about ten minutes I knock it off and raise my arms
like I was getting it straight from the Great Spirit,
"Your new home wants to be here."

I give them time to think about that,
then go, "You'll want the back of your dwelling
to be fairly close to the woods, so you'll have
contact with the bird life. A feeder back there
will draw them from the cover beautifully.
From time to time, you'll see deer, too." Notice
I don't mention the deer ticks. No sense
complicating the simple life.

About that time they're smiling at each other.
Later, after construction starts, they'll be at
each other's throats with cheese spreaders.
But now, while we're still talking, I say,
"Congratulations. You've chosen a lovely site.
You'll want to utilize this excellent southern
exposure, so I recommend we install at least
one good-size bay window, maximize solar collection.
Plenty of warmth and light in your new home.

Your entrance should face the road, so it's
friendly and welcoming, though this deep
on your land you'll have privacy, too,
and reduce road noise." Makes them think
the natives will be coming by to drop off
the free lobsters. I picked some of this stuff up
from those TV carpenter shows, guys
in eighty-dollar designer shirts and tailored
jeans spending millions to make it look simple.

The rest I borrowed from old John Slade.
First time I saw him do that walk-about
on a job site, tugging on his ear, studying the sun,
stepping off the footprint, I knew I was working
for a genius. Clients ate it up, that and John
letting them buy him drinks: "Nothing
these New York fellas want more than
hobnobbing with a genuine Cape Codder
over a platter of Wellfleet oysters, boy.

Tell them a few local stories, you can whip
the wallets out their pockets and tup their women
under their noses, finest kind," he'd say.
"'Course they don't want another nail driven
in town once their house is finished, nor
a supermarket or traffic light, so they can tell
their friends to home how rough they live all summer,

and we can eat Spam and Wonder Bread from
Labor Day to the Fourth of July. So what the hell
do they need insulation for? If they ain't going
to be here when it's cold, I ain't going to give
them any." I'll never forget the day a client
complained about rain getting in around
his trapezoid windows, and old John
got started, "Well, a house is a lot like a boat . . ."

A Reliquary

Soaking and tilting the woods, a storm
too late in the year to be named
drew offshore for the Maritimes, and I went out
walking the wrack line for whatever
rarity might have churned up—

a boat handpump once, workable after
I knocked the dried sand from it,
and once an albatross
driven broken-winged over the dunes,
which I found in the white mat of itself days later
and verified by its four-inch tubenose.

Where the river has shifted its bed
like a whipcrack in an eon of slow motion
between two high dunes, I came on
a patch of ground that water and wind
had cleared as smoothly as a glove
sweeps snow off a windshield.

It looked like wet asphalt on forty feet
of road lightly sanded. I dared not walk on it,
but stood to its side, seeing it was
a stretch of peat with horseshoe patterns
among wheel tracks, and larger hooves,
probably of oxen, then a few boot prints:

whoever had driven those wagonloads of fish
pitchforked off the trapboats in the river,
and the carts piled with salt hay,
would have ridden, mostly, adding weight
to impressions the peat took and kept.

Orlando Shaw or Phil Ryder, I might have
guessed, names on an old map, though few are
remembered by name here, more by their

back-and-forth traffic on cart roads
from cellar hole to cellar hole,
paths to the kettle ponds, a hillside midden
of sea-clam shells, and in layers the next
anonymous wind tucks back into the berm.

II

Horse of Chernobyl, Horse of Lascaux

1. Red Horses

The black I could scavenge from char
around the edge of any firepit, but not the red:
the old man my teacher pointed me across
the flatlands and forest to where a long
cloud hung, below it the mountains
like teeth broken and ground down from
chewing hides to soften them up. The elder
would tell me no more, I understood.
Finding the red rocks was my first duty,
a walk alone into those mountains,
going the trample-way of bison
humping along in their dust, no danger
unless they suddenly turned.

Then I'd be running so fast I would feel
what bound my thighs to my bones
beginning to split and tear. Only a rock
large enough to climb or crouch behind
would keep me from sprinting all the way
out of my skin. Still, I had no idea to fail.
Antelope, too, were on those plains, dancing
away in leap-flow and gallop and leap-flow,
streaming herds I watched with envy.

I wished for that grace when, bellowing in the dark,
its back like a heap of boulders, something
would startle me to a sprint until its noise
was far behind me in the night. I'd run and rest,
pace myself, a man's way, not a thick-necked stallion's
heading up his gathering of mares and young,
with always one horse watching, ears alert, shy
of intruders and snorting fear through its pale muzzle
so the herd reels after the stallion and is gone.
Runners impossible to catch, unless one
straying alone, fine in its stiff black mane

above red-gold girth, pale undercoat, black tail
and legs, lets down its guard, its bulging jowls
working deep in the grass, unaware of spearmen.

The peaks and rock-loose paths by day made me
wish I was back on that plain avoiding the beasts.
I envied hunting birds whose open wings could
take them from height to height without fear that
what they gripped would break off and carry them
down with it. Where were the red stones? I would stop
when I had to take my breath back, sit if I could,
then go on, maybe cross a narrow ledge over
a gorge, the while telling myself to look only
as far down as my two feet. Before dark I would find
one of those small grassy meadows growing
among the crags and wait out the night there.

In the cold towards evening a few goats
might emerge from hiding into the meadow,
white in the gathering dark, each climbing
to a higher place, listening, sniffing the air,
taking time to be sure they were alone. I had rubbed
myself with the earth of the place, a hunter's trick.
When they grazed, their tails swished with pleasure.
I would ask its forgiveness and thank the one
I had chosen before my spear flew. Then the rest
would be gone, leaping down ledge to ledge,
sure-footed, their hooves sounding like
rocks in a clatter on the stone below.

On the fourth sunrise, I saw a red band
as if smeared across a wallface, approachable
after I picked my way up a slide of rubble.
Small pieces lay about the place, crumbling,
and powdered my hands red when I rubbed
them together. Those I returned to our fires with,
running and resting, then up again on my feet,
glad to be gone from those mountains.

Before they went to the fire I scraped the clotted blood
off the next raw chunks of horsemeat, the other
hunters nodding, knowing, and gathered more
powdered blood from the thick horsehide
before the women took their antler scrapers to it.
Where the cave was I knew, but not my place in it.
Though the old man had taught me all
I would need to carry out the test, he couldn't
smooth away my fears, even if he guessed them.
On the night of a horned moon he gave me
a shove, "Go. Go now." In my pouch I packed
dried meat, flints, kindling and split pitchwood,
stone cups, lamps, wicks and tallow. And bladders:
one of water, one of charcoal, one of the red rock powder,
another of powdered horseblood, the pouch
a weight now, to which I added with care
the long hollow wingbone of a crow.

My first time in that dark was a stumble,
sightless as the old man required. I had planned
to make one step, thinking it out before the next,
but as I trailed a hand along the wall, touching its
lumps and damps, at times dripped upon from above,
my hair and shoulders wet, I knew that twisting cave
was leading me, had swallowed me as though it was
a gullet, and was stubbing my feet on its stones
to warn me this would not be easy. The cave
had hung stone teeth like spearheads and cutters
where I would have to crouch or flatten
to avoid tearing my flesh, and at times dropped
its path from under me so I cried out to no one
but my own voice returning from farther places,
a reminder I was even more alone
than in those mountains, not even a goat in sight,
the cave taking me deeper down into the under-earth,
leading me to walls where I had to turn
and retrace my steps, and where on my back sometimes
I'd push through openings with my feet,

hoping not to touch fur or a flinch of scales with one hand
feeling about ahead, the other clutching the pouch.

That old man had sent me weaponless into that dark,
advising I'd know my place when I found it,
but with so much to discover, what would make me
certain? And why not just make fire, for who would see?
Only those watchers from the wall's other side.
A finger slipping into a hole stopped me. Was it here,
or was I too worked up to pursue it further on into the cave's
turnings? Upright, facing the wall I couldn't see,
I set my pouch with care at my feet and felt around,
keeping that finger knuckle-deep in stone
as though that cold spot was the source
of everything. Then I let go and struck fire,
lit one stone lamp and another, set them about
the floor and ignited more, then a torch.

I was not the first. Others had endured the cave's
misleadings and crawls. On the wall, red horses,
some huge as bison, others like mice,
going in all directions of the wind, none paired,
the smaller painted on the larger, the larger
passing through each other as though
there were no such thing as flesh. Deer too,
antlered like trees, and horned bulls, cows, bison,
antelope running beneath them, the wall
like a plain of beasts, some I have never seen,
perhaps no one has seen, but all in a gallop,
yet not fearful I saw as I stared, but as if
a strength beyond them ran through every one.

Wherever I moved, the flickering made them fade,
or seem to come forward out of the stone. I saw
in the various bison humps and horns,
the thick horse necks, the smaller heads or bigger,
the jaws sometimes outsized, the work of many hands.
The legs at times were trailings off of paint, the red shading

strong, or on some beasts almost sandy or brown,
they ran as though on sky—no finger had done
a tree or bush or stream on that wall.

The hole my finger found was perfect for my stallion's eye.
I had thought so in the dark, and it was true by firelight.
I crouched beneath it and stirred red earth and dry horse blood
in a stone cup with water, then sipped, less fearful
of the taste than swallowing the mixture. That would mean
my death, as the old man had warned me. From such mistakes
others had sickened and withered like grass in the sun.

That first mouthful I blew through the crow's bone
around my stallion's eye. The next and next I blew along
his flanks and where I saw his belly would hang.
The neck then, and across the straight back,
then one solid puff to set the rump. While I rinsed
as the old man had shown me, and spat out
the remains of that mixture until no red showed,
I studied my horse so far. Letting it dry, I prepared
in mind to surround those splatters with its form,
the difficult step, ear-points drawn by fingers
in wet charcoal, the black bristle of short mane
thumb-smeared on, thin finger-line for belly and back.
I would have him with tail arched and legs alive in flight.
Or else I could never return there to outline my horse
with a sharp stone when I needed its help for the race
or fight or hunt or the gathering of women. I wanted him
quick to bump and bite, to strike out with a hoof,
his alertness that could not be fooled.

2. Przhevalsky
1886

The trustworthy Poliakov measured
the bone cask of the skull in St. Petersburg,
studying details of its jaws, teeth
and eye sockets, comparing other equines,

and concluded that the pelt and skull
I was presented with in Mongolia were not
an extinct tarpan's, but of another unknown
wild horse, larger and also extinct.
Except that the reddish woolly winter coat
was a sure marker: in several
Mongolian habitats I had seen these
squarely built, shaggy beauties
on the hoof—once while crossing Dzungaria,
other times at the oasis Gashun Nor,
small gatherings of mares and young
led by a stallion. He was always in motion,
nervously aware, shaking head and tail,
raising his nostrils to the wind like
a hunting dog. They would scent us
almost a mile away and gallop
out of sight in a single file,
the stallion circling his herd, quick
to nudge any lagging foal or mare.

The skull was a tarpan's or khulan's
or another breed of wild ass, insisted
some gentlemen who never left their desks
at the Academy, and certainly not
to set foot in that lost world of the Gobi,
in Mongol *a waterless barren grassless plain.*
And empty, scoured to bone-colored gravel
by the snow, then wind, then rain, and sun-baked,
saline, treeless, slashed into cross-hatchings
of gullies and ravines, as though its creator
was a mad ploughman. Look before you
or behind and it was the same, a disorientation
so profound it seemed you could see the earth
curving away in front of your eyes.
Imagine the boredom. Any wonder that
out of such burnt and frozen steppes
enclosed by mountains
came centuries of short, wide,

bowlegged nomads made for horseback,
their broad faces tanned to leather,
slit-eyed from riding into the elements:
Huns, Avars, Magyars, Tamerlane,
Chingis Khan. And why not climb
into a wooden saddle and head off
south or west for the gates of Baghdad
or the Balkans? Anywhere for
a leafy grove enveloping
shade and coolness, a sky free enough
of dust to display its colors, or to verify
the rumor of an ocean. To keep
those Mongol horsemen out
the Chinese built their Great Wall.

If you judge a man by how well
he sits a horse, none is better than
a Mongol. If only one of them could get
a rope on a *takhi,* that wild horse
of their country, whose name
means *spirit.* As for a wooden saddle,
don't bother. I've heard that horse
will roll it to splinters. I have at Sloboda
cases of specimens, even a stuffed
Tibetan bear and a signed portrait of
the Tsarevich. I would bargain them all
for a breeding pair of *takhi* to feed on the grass
of my estate. Not a robe, not a pile of bones
I might bring down with a rifle. Those horses
deserve better for the way they endure
that Gobi weather, the night frosts into May,
then northwesterly gales that will
peel back on occasion ages of sand
to reveal silver dishes and other
treasure. Though I have never set eyes
on evidence of such buried cities,
not even as a man of science
and a soldier would I tempt death—

which the Mongols say comes quickly
after laying a hand on such items.

Cold, salt, sand and dust, twilight
at morning, even the Bactrian camels
shutting down, closing their eyes
and noses, turning their rumps on it,
refusing to go on. Then summer
and by noon that desert visibly
smoking like a brick stove. The wild
horse tracks—if that's what they were—
would swim in our sight, and our strength
leak away with our pouring sweat. Even
the camels perspired, tongues hanging
like a dog's, and not a word passed
among the caravan, as though
to speak might rupture
our aching brains. We were
a mechanism moving without sound
toward the hope of evening,
and the hoofprints would vanish
as though into air, as though
to demonstrate that the wind's shape
is a *takhi*'s shape. Meanwhile,
in St. Petersburg they'd be saying,
General Przhevalsky is seeing things again!

Still, better the Gobi than a city where
the atmosphere in a room is colder
than on any steppe. Since we are speaking of
camels who can drink thirty gallons of water
in ten minutes, I swear I have observed
men at dinner attempting the same,
albeit with sterner liquids, and ladies
in the grand ballrooms with eyelashes
drawn out and painted to such lengths
as to outdo the functional
double-rowed lashes of the Bactrians,

and tougher mouths, for though
a camel will chew thorns when hungry,
it has breeding enough never to spit
the sharp points at the turned backs of its kind.

Nor can you admire black-tailed gazelles
in St. Petersburg, or the seldom encountered
Marco Polo sheep, or come upon a
puddle-sized oasis surrounded in August
by pink blossoms of *Hedysarum*. Mongolia
is legendary too for the rapacity
of its crows, which Mongols will not dispatch
because they consider it wrong
to kill birds. Therefore black flocks
will follow a caravan across the desert
as thickly as gulls trouble the air
at the stern of a fishing boat on the sea.
They perch on camels and steal rusks
from sacks of provisions, even tear
into the humps of their grazing victims
until they elicit screams. Shoot the thieves
and others soon appear to take up their positions.

It provokes a question: Mongols or crows,
which taught which to steal?
For as well as bent on misdirection
when asked the way to such-and-such
or where the *takhi* herds might be found,
a Mongol can be quick-fingered
around your property. That I was
the Tsar's general meant nothing,
so they needed to see my skill at
bringing down birds in flight
or dropping a distant antelope.
Sometimes only viewing a gun
would suffice. I learned to assume
that my guide was a spy, always,
and when making notes or taking down

bearings would arrange beforehand
for one of my companions to create
some distraction. In this the compass
and field glasses often took part,
as the guides had trouble distinguishing
one from the other, and were dazzled by
the mysteries of both. Look in one end
and the scene was far away, look in
the other and it was near. But in neither end
would I see a wild horse close enough
for a rope. And that compass needle,
was it alive? That is how we locate the animals,
I'd assure the guides, who upon reflection
kept their own mysteries, and knew
what animal it couldn't locate.

3. Zone of Alienation

Tuteshni, we call ourselves, "locals,"
but to the Zone's watchdogs we are *samosels,*
"squatters," by which they mean vagrants,
scavengers and thieves, though these were
our fields and villages before their reactor
coughed up three Hiroshimas a day
for more than a week. Cesium, iodine, lead,
cadmium, berillium, barium, weapons-grade
plutonium—you name it, we had it
dumped on us, four hundred and fifty
varieties of radionuclides. How well
I remember that first rain afterwards,
the droplets pilling and joining like mercury.
And the puddles—here green, there
yellow as sunflowers. And they claim
radiation has no color? The truth
came later, of course, after the government
had buried it as they buried the cats and dogs,
hosed down and flattened cars and houses
and pushed them into pits. Someone

sometime will have to enumerate to God
what's buried under this country. But the truth
is like grass—given enough time it climbs from
its grave. We were fenced out even after
they buried Reactor Four and renamed it
the Sarcophagus. We lived in cities like Kiev,
where *Chernobyl,* whispered behind a hand,
made people have to be someplace else in a hurry.
As if after dark we lit up like neon tubes. As if
we had partaken of those mushrooms
rumored to be the size of human heads,
and lived where flies could turn the doorknobs
and walk in. Those days the newspapers
were full of stories—hairless hedgehogs,
packs of chickens killing the foxes.
Until I decided, better to deal with such
mutations than to remain there
and be treated like a horror-film vampire.
Besides, I missed the lucky signs of storks
on rooftops, and woke each night—Thank God
not shining in the dark!—from dreaming of
this house and of tending to this garden here.
I came back under the fence and into the leaves
through the forest one night, no militia anywhere.
Even they had been officially economized.
I had to see if home still existed, to satisfy
a persistent nudge I had that the administrators
had outspent the plan before the finish line
was in sight. In the old cemetery among the trees,
I stopped to visit my mother and father.

This house was a husk then, even the doors
and windows stolen, the stove stolen, my books—
I was a schoolteacher when there were
children here. From nothing will come
something, then? I asked the sky,
and that time for once got a quick answer:
a heavy rain that proved the roof was good.

Even the sparrows were gone, as though
whatever moved had been pocketed
by thieves, even the flowers. It was two years
before someone passing shouted from the road,
I saw a sparrow taking a bath in the dust!
I had turned looter myself, a nightly visitor
to remains of other houses and farms
for whatever I needed to live here.
Nature's revenge, I saw it all. Moss breaking
the asphalt down to grit; pines, birches,
and willows popping the pavements, ripping
with knuckled roots, baring soil for
new growth. Whole fields of lavender asters.

On paper no one lives here. But the Zone managers
are officious aunties, and need to know what everyone's
up to. Once in a while they even deliver the mail
and check my vegetables with dosimeters.
Turns out we *tuteshni* get double the dosages of
outside folks, but look! I could fall and break my neck.
Those who stayed away in cities or shabby camps
have suffered worse. Hypochondriacs, convinced with
every scratch they've contracted Death.
Madness everywhere! Brawling in mud streets!
Here the bus carries me to markets in the city
once a month. More than enough. Doctors poke me
and shine lights in my eyes and check me off
on their clipboards from time to time.

One morning just over there a wolf stood in the road,
a look on his face as if to say, Well, squatter,
what shall we do with this bumbledump
technology has made for us? All the animals
were coming back. Boars running in packs
like the revenge of pigs fenced in forever.
They are our mastodons, and I soon learned
to pick fruit early and keep out of
abandoned orchards after the windfalls

started, lest one of those barreling porkers
collide with me and snap my legs like twigs.
Black storks are thriving, though rare
before the fallout. I was living in a sanctuary
for wildlife and had soon fallen in love
with the silence, birdsong its only punctuation,
or the barking of a lynx back in the trees.
The sound of a vehicle brings Kiev
back in a hurry. As for mutations, the new pines
are dwarfed into bushes, and on their normal limbs
some of the chestnuts sprout huge leaves,
but among the fauna only barn swallows were
changed that I could see, their faces albino-spotted.

That statue of Lenin you passed as you came in,
did you notice? One hand in his pocket, one grasping
his lapel as if he had a plan? Each time I pass him
I ask, "What surprise do you have for us today,
Comrade? Or are you too busy in Hell?"
One morning, a few patches away from
that great thinker, the surprise was there,
nibbling the grass. A horse, a small,
copper-colored horse, little taller than a pony,
but blocky, sturdier looking. The jaw seemed
prehistoric, a huge working lump, designed
for a bigger animal, and the extremities
were black, legs, tail, even the mane that stood up
like the short bristles on a pushbroom.
At last I have seen a four-legged mutation, I thought.
Because no work horse of this country—
most now mere underground arrangements
of bones, buried with the rusalkas,
those sirens who stole men's souls—was that
straight-backed and compact. As I walked
slowly away, it stared but kept on chomping.
Later from the postman I learned that
small herds had been trucked in to give them
breeding room and let them eat the irradiated

grass and stomp it out with their hooves. The last
wild horses on Earth, brought from the plains
of Mongolia to the estate at Askania Nova
a hundred years ago, fewer left now in this world
than us *tuteshni*. Tough Przhevalsky's horses,
able to live in cold conditions like ours. Dead Zone?
One day there may be thousands here. Wolves
they treat like soccer balls. Like us
they are foragers, and need wide territory
between them and the other herds. Too smart
to be tamed or ridden. Kick and bite,
snap and spin is their way, even among
themselves, as I have seen since Lenin showed me
the first one. Here, drink a glass with me
before you go. "For the horse," as we *tuteshni* say.
No fear, it's made with sugar I get from
the mobile shop in exchange for my potatoes.
A glass of this and you'll feel the roentgens
and becquerels fly away.

These Little Town Blues

1. How Chief McHugh Got His Birdwatching Gear

Whenever this little video of the Rev. Italo Parisi
and his merry band of Charismatics—including
my ex-wife, Margie—starts running in my head,
I haul the binoculars or scope out and scour
Tautog Creek down there under the station window.
Not that I'm wild about the birds, but they're
sure a diversion from the humans I deal with
day to day. Even Margie could turn up in town,
since sooner or later everyone comes to Cape Cod.
I can see Rev. Parisi in bermuda shorts and a shirt
with a little alligator on it, touristy but given away
by the shiny black shoes and black socks, looking
even more like Omar Sharif than he does
in a roman collar. He pulls his black Buick
to the curb on Main Street and opens the doors
for Margie and three other women, middle-aged,
gotten up like vacationers in tennis visors, sandals
and wraparound skirts. Then he leads them
into the drugstore, where all five crowd
the condom display, screening it, and begin
driving hatpins into the packaging. Am I bitter?
That's what I wonder as I reach into the desk
for my Zeiss binoculars—not mine exactly,
but on long-term loan from Wilber McCandless,
as is that scope on the tripod by the window. It wasn't
just that Wilber liked to look out his own window
with them: he liked to do it after dark from his cupola
overlooking Commercial Street, the one
his great-grandad Capt. Miciah had put there
so his wife could climb up and watch for
his slow return with whale oil every few years
from the Bering Sea or South Atlantic. The 360
degree vista of temptations that glassed-in room
afforded Wilber was no place for a nice boy of forty-six
to be spending his evenings. Lucky his mom

recognized that before someone outside the family
discovered him up there so close to the stars.
When she came to me our charitable conclusion was
to confiscate the offending lenses. "Hope you told her
to stitch up his pockets, too," my foul-minded
sergeant Crocker Newton said.

2. Sgt. Crocker Newton on the Usual Suspects

New Age lizards, washashores, blow-ins,
if they're loose they roll to Cape Cod
any time the country tilts this way,
because Florida's too far, too big a drain
on their concentration. Not to mention
the one-to-a-crate originals
already present and accounted for—
the homegrowns dealing joints and coke
out of their rides at beach parking lots,
probationers and marginal offenders
we invite to the station for a sit-down.

I look at them and think: *hapless.*
That's the word I drag the bottom of
my vocabulary for, and brother, it fits.
I've toured the fifty states, and this place
right here is breathtaking. But do they see it?
Too interested in bodily harm. What good's
fresh air when you can have a spider web—
with spider—tattooed between your thumb
and index finger? That young lady with
a swallow on each ankle and a bear's footprint,
claws and all, on her ample calf? You ever
wonder how they'll explain those items
to the grandkids forty years from now,
after time and fat and sagging muscle,
bad habits and cellulite?

Mostly it's in the eyes, though, lack of—what?
Fire? Energy? Like they were fed as kids

on test cereals that didn't make the grade.
Remember those colored puffs and corkscrews,
looked like pictures of germs they show
on the mouthwash commercials now?
And don't get me started on the shoes.
Cowboy boots aren't functional for work
or leisure in Cape Cod sand, and the women
in clunkers that look like milled chunks
of 2 x 4, or those over-the-knee spiked boots
like Errol Flynn wore in *Captain Blood*.
Less than a mile of sidewalk in this town,
so they must spend their lives in cars, their kids
raised on Sunoco fumes and Fritos.

Multiple earrings, nose and tongue studs,
eyebrow rings. Call me crazy, but I'd hide
in the cellar during lightning storms.
I'd be afraid to pass the refrigerator, for fear
I'd end up on the door with the magnets.
I blame all this self-mutilation on the death
of Communism. Now we take out our aggressions
with road rage, public provocations over nothing,
and driving to New Bedford to pay total strangers
big bucks to shoot us full of holes so's we can
walk around hung with hardware.
Had Cole Farjohn in the station last week,
had a beercan pop-top through his nose,
it looked like. Christ, Cole, I said, be careful
with that thing around coathangers.
You're liable to find you hung
your schnozzola in the closet.

3. Sgt. Newton Recollects the Return of Thane Gould
   to Endicott, Massachusetts, in the Winter of 1977

That was the winter a nameless December hurricane
laid the freighter *Etruria* lengthwise on the sand
at Head of the Meadow, then Thane appeared

in early January as though there was some connection,
hitchhiking down Route 6. Before I saw who it was
I had already pulled the cruiser over to check him out:
short on luggage, jailhouse tattoos on the back
of his hands, hair to his shoulders and stiff as
peanut brittle, like you could snap it off. And his back
showing signs of defeat, still lugging the invisible piano
of a recent attitude adjustment. A cop's inclination
is to keep a vision like that moving on down the road:
he's probably not in town to visit his dear old mother.
Then I saw it was Cousin Thane, only thinner than
chopsticks and fresh from two years' incarceration
down there in Santa Marijuana or whatever they call it.
Before I let him off at Aunt Shirley's, he'd told me
what a damn fool he was. Gone and gotten in on the deal
because he wanted to go into auto parts, twenty K
they promised him and the other guys apiece on delivery
of the bales up here to Cape Cod, except by the time
they'd anchored overnight at Santa Whatchacallit
the crew was sampling the cargo, and everyone
in port got wind of it. The jailer'd slide a bowl into the cell
and watch them fight for it like chickens in a henyard.
Fish and rice the whole two years. Of course the pusbags
who'd signed him up went into thin air, and the moral
of the story is that when Thane did the math—plenty of time
for that between eye-gougings for a few mackerel parts—
he saw he could have saved the twenty grand
by doing oil changes right here in Endicott two years
for Moxie Hogan, or shingling for the Olafsen brothers.
He's been clean ever since. Chopping up the beams
and laths in the house Aunt Shirley left him
to keep warm was dumb, but it wasn't a crime.
All night he leaves the lights on in that little trailer,
even now. Says he gets dizzy in strange buildings.
Things couldn't been too easy in that jailhouse after dark,
I'd say, and anyway a man's got to watch himself.

4. Sgt. Newton and the Crows

I used to admire the way they'd stand two feet
from traffic, ripping away at a roadkill. It showed
some grit and independence, even performed
a civic duty, policing the highway. That afternoon
I heard them before I saw them, and thought
they'd treed an owl or hawk the way they do.
A ways further down High Barbary Road
I saw them, roosting and flapping around
on Cole Farjohn's scalloper, that floating eyesore
the *Lady Evelyn,* up on blocks and peeling paint
by the road side, probably named for some
down-cape pushover Farjohn thought he was
in love with. A couple dozen crows were up
in the rigging and goose-stepping along
the gunnels, on the pilot house roof—except
I wouldn't call the glorified phone booth
Farjohn has up there a pilot house—
and dropping down onto the deck, flying off
into the trees and coming back. I should have known
by then. Some men have their deaths written
all over them and Cole was one, the Bad Year Blimp,
as Earl Seed down at the Bunker called him. Then
I caught the smell. Farjohn dumping shells
and gurry in the bushes? OK, we'd add that
to the charges. I still wasn't getting the picture,
and when I pulled up next the boat the crows
blasted off into the woods. When I got out
to look around, it was no question of inhaling.
My breath got as far as my molars and backed off.
Nothing under the hull, nothing in the woods but pines
and crows. Farjohn's old tank of a Pontiac was parked
at his house up the road, widow-maker of a place,
tarpaper held down by laths, a tin stovepipe
elbowed out the wall, capped about two feet from
the roofline, and go ahead, ask me if he burned pine.

Ask me if we took a 9 mm Glock pistol out of his freezer
after the Mid-Cape Electronics break-in. But the stink?
No way without a ladder I could get on deck.
I opened my passenger door and stood up there.
Not high enough, so I climbed over
the bumper onto the hood, thinking, Chief's
going to ream me out if I put a dent in it.
When I stood full height and looked
into the deck area, all I could think of
was how Cole kept a couple of tortoiseshell
pussycats at his place, and had such tiny feet
for a large man, then I wrapped both arms
around myself and doubled up.

5. Sgt. Newton's Indie Film Debut

Endicott, Massachusetts, is turning up
on the silver screen a trifle too often, if you ask me.
Chamber of Commerce loves it, film school graduates
shooting their own scripts in town, budgets so low
they don't get past the premiere here at the Rialto,
or maybe onto Cable 6 plus an interview
with your host Jack Cole. The story's always
about film school graduates maxing out their plastic
making movies while their parents ride their backs
about attending law school. What's wrong with
this picture? Mirrors within mirrors, that's what.
So their girlfriends get to chew the local scenery
as female leads, and some of our more
photogenic citizens get to leer from the dark
into windows and such—Les Kraft and Arthur Swain
are lately talking Actors' Equity. But cut to the action
yesterday morning: some of the fishermen
got down the wharf to go out scalloping and found it
roped off. These kids had selectmen's OK to work
on town property, provided there wasn't any nudity.
So Fred Bunjoe and Bobby Collery and the others
are sitting in their pickups thinking, There goes

another day of fishing. Meanwhile this couple's
down the wharf pretending to have an argument.
Kid with a hand-held camera's bouncing around them
getting all the angles and another's holding a mike
on a boom over their heads, and here comes old
Bill Coehlo going about twenty, driving
right for the rope and dragging it and a sawhorse
on either end down the wharf. Next thing the others
are following, offloading gear in the midst of the scene.
The kid director's wearing one of those Australian
cowboy hats. One side of the brim pinned up
against the crown the way they do? Only now
he's got a whistle in his mouth and running
and waving his arms like a referee, trying
to get the boys back in their trucks. Bob Chisholm
sticks a leg out and trips the kid so's the whistle
when he hits the wharf breaks several front teeth.
About the time I got there, the kid's mouth
looks like the entrance to the Ted Williams Tunnel.
Bob Chisholm's being sued for damages:
cameraman kept shooting as the trucks came down—
catch the realism, I guess—so there's Bob's foot
as the kid ran past and I'm in it too, me and
Bill Walker trying to calm everybody down. Now
they want to work us all into the plot, serendipity
the camera guy calls it. First time in all my years
of policework I debated pulling my weapon
or not on folks I've known my whole life.

6. Moxie Hogan's Alibi
as heard by Chief McHugh

It was never any use telling him, Just
give it to me straight, and this time
he was less than a non sequitur into
his whereabouts on the night
in question when I remembered
Myles O'Malley, the Tin Whistle King,

a little man with a squarish head,
irregularly toothed, like a carved stump
dredged from a Mayo bog, who stood
on the sidewalk behind his hat
streeling and threaping through
his instrument when I was a kid,
sounds I later discovered
from my reading in Irish history
were the equivalents of a vortex
disappearing into itself, a circle
pecked in a stone that might turn up
at the entrance to New Grange,
or the whole tinny unloading
of a hoard of torcs and collars,
because we Hogans, O'Malleys
and McHughs had moved too often
across time, from Asia all the way
to offshore Europe, so we longed at
some level for continuance, the omphalos
of home as the scholars I read to chill
out of this job put it, rounds like
the Tara earthworks, rings like
the Drombeg Stones, to be reeled
and wrangled around because here at last
was a center for our world—hence Moxie's
diddling with the facts, more lullaby
than alibi, but not that, either: less text
than marginalia, like those drawn-out
beasts with their occasional
triadic heads representing
Moxie's version, the law's, and the truth.

IV

Around Master Williams

Roger Williams, 1604?–1683
Founder of Providence Plantation
and the colony of Rhode Island

1. The Snow Trial
Winter 1636

There are mornings when that cold reaches up
through the years for me, and clamps a hand
from underground about my arch, and days
even in summer when the memory of that snow
will drift against this hip, hunting my marrow,
until I ask, *How does this burning differ from that*
in my fireplace over there? When I turned
from Mary and the children in our Salem doorway
and saw as if for the first time whiteness without
a footprint in every direction, what moment
worse? Unless to be braced in irons and shoved
onto a deck at Nantasket, as the Bay Colony
intended, and returned as a criminous heretic
to England and Bishop Laud, the inquisitor
who drove me here. Bearskin coat,
pack on my back, I turned southwestward
as my compass, already cold, pointed the way.
The weather of that year had prefigured
its fierceness with a great blow the August before,
wherein many died and stories abounded
of pinnaces driven to plow cornfields. I saw
for myself whole forests laid sideways each
upon another. One night on my journey I woke
to a fresh snow climbing into a ghostly pallor,
enwrapping the figure of my enemy John Cotton.
He aimed a finger, saying, "Roger Williams,
Separatist, do not dare imagine that you are
the Ram's Horn of the true and living God. That
is a snare of wickedness. So too your claim
that a magistrate cannot punish sins against

the first tablet of the Commandments."
Then the breeze lifted him shining off between
the black trunks in those woods. How far
above my head the streams I waded into
had risen, running with snowmelt, I could never
judge beforehand. Though taller than now,
never was I of middling height. Thus it is no
figure of speech to me, that phrase *swept away,*
but one full of tumbles and ice clutter,
cold boilings and soaks. Southwest as my compass
showed me, always southwest, toward where
the Indians say their heaven *Sowwanaiu* awaits
after death, though I hoped I was headed only as far
as Massasoit's country, those swamps out of the wind
where his Wampanoags held out against winter.
My feet printing the silences had become a sign
of my dismay. Bedless, without bread,
one morning in the troughs a night wind
had wormed through a storm, I came upon two quail.
Their dead-grass yellowish throats and eyestreaks,
colors of winter oakleaf and snow-striped branches
were no defense in that white world of red-tailed hawks
and red-legged wolves—the wolves I would sense
before I saw, trailing me at a distance, faces
locked in concern at my intrusion on their wilderness.
Taking aim, the mere threat of a shot would send them
fading back into the landscape without hurry. But
these quail. Their brushy coverts were buried
under that weather: I never thought of them as food.
As though they understood me their last hope of succor,
they did not fly into that absence rumbling
through the land. I sat on a deadfall
doling them parched corn out of my pack,
feeding those querking birds though I could not
provide for my family and home out of a stiff neck
and high-handedness that led me ever from contention
into dispute. Between prayers I accused my own pride.
Because of me, Mary and our children had not even

a handful of feathers to defend their heartbeats
against the worser human cold of Salem. Moon
upon snow, snow against sun, a thickening of the air
coming across distance, and I was like a pebble again,
sorely tossed in the flow, and in the dark,
John Cotton—"You obstruct God's holy will and law.
Mend yourself. Return to Salem and show
your neighbors the proper penitence."
That time I swept his accusings from the air
with my oak staff. "Be off, you flea of rectitude,"
I told that swirling wraith in my waking sleep,
and heard my quaking voice for the first time
in all those days without calendar. Then the wind
announcing my erasure under the million
wobbling stars again, and I a black clot moving
southwest as the cold button of the compass
I tried to warm in my hands showed me. In those places
that were no place, my mouth bearded with ice,
breath falling as crystals on the bear's fur,
the fire gone out again, I saw myself as
a grateful beast descending in that fur into pastures
restored to spring, to drink from waters purling
but calm, a place at last I had no wish to return from
or pass by. There, after long sleep, I would settle
my little family. But *Roger Williams, What cheer?*
What cheer, Nétop? The hands of Massasoit's people
drew me away from that kindly dying, and led me
step by warming step to a cave under the hill,
where hot stones would try to bake that cold
out of me, bringing me back to the smell of mud,
and skunk cabbage melting its way out of old snow.

2. Letter from George Ludlow, Merchant, to Roger Williams
   October, 1637

My dear worthy friend, I write in the hope that my letter
finds you in prosperity and peace. Since last I wrote
I have delivered twelve pounds sterling to Mr. Coggeshall

for the goods I had of you to sell at Virginia this year past.
Please be apprised that those sums which you request
of me are skewed, therefore. In lieu of the three goats
I should have given you for your watch, I have paid
to Mr. Mayhew eight pounds, thus freeing you
of obligation to both gentlemen. As to that other watch,
which you sharply overvalue at thirty to forty shillings,
though pretty it is a laggard timekeeper, as with most
house watches of its kind, and could not charm
a purchaser. You shall have it in hand the next spring,
as I deposited it so far up the country there's no returning
along that hard shore until the weather breaks for
planting time. As you so ordered, I brought four score
weight of tobacco, but alas our bark took to the bottom
with a leak, spoiling that cargo and much more of my own.
Such be the hazards of a merchant's life. Lord willing,
we shall have a better year ahead, and profit the both of us,
and you shall have tobacco of me then. By reason of
my aforesaid great losses I could not bring the heifer,
which of itself and all above is no call to resort to attorneys,
for through my endeavors you will be satisfied next year
with payment in kind or else in corn. God and a fair ship
willing, you will see me plying your Narragansett waters
a day in June or April, to spell out to your face our situation—
even to the whereabouts of Mrs. Williams's gown new come
from England—in words acuter than this unschooled hand
can manage, whose owner wishes you all health,
and health to your fine family—which persons stir
my admiration of you—and promises with all respective
salutations that I shall deal as true with you as with another.

3. Samuel Gorton: Letter of Roger Williams to William Blackstone
Providence, 1644

Days ago, passing through Shawomet
into the Narragansett country, I heard
or thought I heard a conversation

among the trees, one of those times
when the leaves give tongue to a dialect
almost human, and there, at a turn
of the way, that man of gusts and jars
Samuel Gorton, who once I feared
would drive me for a little peace
from Providence all the way to
Patience Island, and make of me
a hermit there, so needful was that man
of a cooler and bridle. One who truly
believed in the indwelling Holy Spirit,
you would suppose, might not be
such a goat for trouble. No heaven
but in good hearts, he preached,
no hell but locked in sinners' minds.
Yet the man's seductive rhetoric
so fanned affrayments as to cause
in meadows and byways near perpetual
brawling, men with oaken clubs at
each other's ears. His turbulent carriages
soon earned him the way to the gate
of every settlement he entered. Driven
from Plymouth for heresy as well as
mutiny, whipped and banished
from Pocasset when his maidservant
assaulted an old woman and he declared
the justices "just Asses." And what a misled
knot of followers he drew with him
to Providence Plantation, and what
some people will believe! Though who
could say these years what he holds true?
Do church and ceremony still obstruct for him
the Spirit's direct entry, as if It were a falcon
stooping on its prey? Have I not myself
taken leave of settlements in the night,
and once by plowing for weeks through
vast snows, because like Samuel Gorton
I questioned an article or two of faith

or government? Don't I believe that health
of spirit is earned in strife and ferment,
but dries to a rattling pod in churches
where none disagrees with another? But
Samuel Gorton poured the gall of satire
into the vinegar of sarcasm, and stirred them,
while I tried persuasion, my reasons
laid out in order like a pedlar his wares.
We both took pride in threats falling upon
our departing shoulders, surely, proof
we were in the right, and there are some
who claim more salutary elements
to his nature, it's true, by which he could
turn a listener's heart whilst preaching
in the Towne Street. I am not one of those,
yet pestilent as he was, he was not the worst
of the barbarous offscourings whom Time
has dragged through Providence.
William Harris, for one, diseased with
land lust, and others of his kind for whom
the common trinity of this world is profit,
preferment, and pleasure, the triumvirate
of God Land, God Belly, and God Gold—
George Ludlow and those Hawkins brothers,
to list but three, who flew from their debts
as wild geese beat south before the snows,
or the womanizer Wright, or divers
grave-robbers and cattle reavers, or Verin
who thrashed his wife because in conscience
she believed otherwise than he, and that
whole tribe of fantasticks, those shakers,
quakers, and self-anointed apostles.
With Samuel Gorton you always knew
what ground you stood upon, and that day
on my path his peace was written on his face
in sunlight falling through the leafage.
Palms outward, as if in tranced acceptance
of whatever he apprehended there—his God?

a delusion of old age?—he spake aloud,
and there was no pretense in his not seeing me
as I passed behind him on my way, touched
as I was. But driven too by the sharp
and bitter arrows he loosed upon us all
when he was resident here, I moved off
quietly as a fox on the ends of my toes.

4. Letter from Roger Williams to John Winthrop, Jr.
Fisher's Island, 1647

Though they are everywhere, in swales and open woods,
by stream banks and marshes, and clothe the soil
against dispersing wind and rain, we rarely admit
the grasses to mind—perhaps we admire a field
of turkeyfoot in its deer-colored autumn transformation,
but forgetting how it will husband the soil beneath it
into sods. Broomsedge, too, invading disturbed grounds
to clump there and take hold. Common hairgrass
and panic grass, rice grass—each is like
a trusted apprentice who goes about his business
without our notice, unless it be in a seasonal change,
as when the Indian grass, tall as a man, puts on
its golden seedhead like a plume in the hat
of an arrant cavalier, or the bunchgrass shows
all winter stems of a darkest red, the seed-tufts
white above. Still other stands may flash foxlike
in sunlight, or a breeze speak its mind through them.
Regarding the forage available on Fisher's Island,
of cattails I have no doubt, and salt-marsh grasses,
not sweet like English fodder, but available in plenty.
Neither these nor the native ryes and broomstraws
I mention will compete with English hays in promoting
the girth and disposition of your beasts, however.
They are rank and coarse, and your livestock may grow
lousy and out of heart, indeed so stringy the wolves
will neglect them, or else so contrary the town's
Viewer of Swine and Cattle will be much at your door.

Therefore these five bushels of English bluegrass
and white clover seed from our fields, heaped
for allowance and shipped from Providence
with Captain Throgmorton, along with my warmest
regards to yourself and your kindest companion.
If you can spare me a little season, permit me a few words
of instruction about this seed: it is best sown
upon a rain preceding, and broadcast three bushels
to an acre, the ground requiring little more beforehand
than the scratching you would give the ear
of your favorite hound. My brother Robert Williams
advises scattering it as soon as received, no matter
the season, and further that you allow the ripe grasses
so to stand that the wind doles and disperses them.
You will find even their husks and the dung of cattle
that feed upon them will cause their increase,
so agreeable to profusion be their crops—though heed
me here: such is their potency that when planted
near an orchard they will usurp its groundwater
as surely as if they were slaking themselves
with the juices of your fruits, drying and puckering
them ere they be plucked from off the bough.

5. Roger Williams's Shipwreck Letter
to the Citizens of Providence Colony
1652

Five times to your one I have crossed that ocean,
citizens, in little more than wormy buckets
fitted out with sails, four of those voyages
in the service of this our colony—hat in hand
whilst seeking in London the patents and protectors
for our endeavor—and discovered full well
each time how the sea will become the sea until
without fail it ceases to be a revel, and yet
returning here, setting foot on this soil,
I am each time met with what it pains me
to designate the common shipwreck of mankind,

yourselves inspiring such gales and blackenings
as no mere ocean could thrash from itself
or support, nor any ship navigate to a peaceable
haven. I speak of this Rhode Island drowning
in disorders of our own creation, tumults
blowing from all the compass points,
each man sailing without a sheet anchor
under the seething wind of his own argument,
division following breach following distraction
as wave follows upon the heels of wave.
Litigations, rumored alliances with the Dutch,
papers of contention, island versus mainland
and self-appointed commission versus
covetous council. Traduction, denunciations
piled one upon another as the tide piles
in broken billows, the civilities of town meeting
reduced to fragments like a shallop dashed
against rocks. Citizens, we have willingly bypassed
the fair wind of a unanimous spirit, and are like
a ship's master tacking and dodging
in a great fog whilst each crewman, claiming
freedom of conscience as a license to select
whatever course best suits his own advancement,
ignores the common weal and woe which binds him
to shipmates and passengers, hauling aloft
or furling whatever foresail or mizzensail he will,
deaf to the master's cries, this as the passengers
refuse to pay their fares, and the forecastle
mutinies against the hold even as all hope
by some blindly benevolent fortune to arrive
safely in harbor. Do you take my metaphor? Look
around. For here on land you will see the shipwreck
sponsored by such policy. Your hogs straying
through your neighbors' gardens, bridges
in disrepair unto collapse for want of adequate
payment of just levies, and for want of a ready
militia, our colony under the measure of
land-greedy eyes at Boston and Plymouth,

and of threatenings to the west,
lurking upon the moment of sunset.

6. Doffing & Donning: An Exchange of Letters
Roger Williams and William Blackstone,
Providence, 1663

RW:
First it was the donning, to be sure,
William Blackstone, then the doffing,
the putting on and pulling off of one's hat,
the doffing in deference to another.
You would think such policy below
the notice of theological gurnippers,
but alas their only business is ever yours.

Once I determined that during church
such doffing was mere self-display,
will-worship, the eyes exalting the body
instead of God, I concluded that for all
the Father of Lights has need of such
affectations we might as well pull
our shoes off, too. And do the like in
public affairs as well, such doffing
and donning before elected officers
as to fawn upon authority, which I had
hoped to shed across the ocean,
and then in the Bay Colony.

But there seems no end to the disputation
about the doffing and donning, for Mr. Coddington
of Aquidneck Island, a brass-faced schemer
who in London had himself appointed governor
of our Aquidneck for life, though shortly
annulled, and had tried to give that island
to Plymouth Colony, was ever resentful
of the trust Rhode Islanders had invested with me.

To be sure the man was a haberdasher of
small questions, and put it about that
I had wavered mightily over the doffing
and the donning because I once suggested
that men should wear caps, not hats, in church.
And lo, who should appear as it were at his shoulder
but Richard Scott, my neighbor of near thirty years,
to swear he had seen me with hat donned
at worship and in civic dealings, and yet
had observed me doffing and donning
to every jack passerby on the Providence street.

So thrive the fleas of rectitude, Dear William,
nor suffer each other to breathe the common air.
There be no action too small to make war
or gossip over. Trip on a root and you're drunk.
Sneeze and you're in the graveward direction.

WB:
I will come riding down from Study Hill
on Ajax, the mouse-colored bull, Dear
Roger Williams, for you appear to need
the counsel of one who survived
the Visible Saints and their holy
flea-skinnings, one who came here
to Rhode Island as you did because
in Boston there is no escaping the agents
of one heavenly side or another.

There, as in the lanes of London,
I have oftimes noted the visible
twitching of an ear toward another's
conversation, the head it adorned
unmoved, though sometimes the eyes
were swiveling about for a better view.
A difficult move to effect, Sir,
as I'm sure you'll agree.

And the lingering assessment over
a shoulder, that too, even in church,
as one inquisitor or another—who doubtless
would claim he sailed for this wilderness
to worship without fear, but in truth was
as morally rigid as an icicle, eager to apply
the hot iron to a cheek, or split a nose—
studied me for a bit of error he could retail
to Bishop Laud, or the Bay Colony elders,
or any authority, and call it God's work.
As if his hand weren't out for preferment.

There be some such heretic hunters even here
in our Rhode Island, as your great doffing
and donning controversy illustrates.
I shall leave the mild Ajax—whom
the Narragansetts deem *great medicine*—
like a civil dog at your door, and we will partake
of a jug of the strong waters, and liven the afternoon
with our laughter, our Greek and Latin
and Hebrew, as when we were boys at Cambridge.
For the laughter of a friend triples one's own.

7. A Proposal of Banishment
Roger Williams, 1669

Unless he be astray in his wits, no man wishes
for increase of wolves, which we have in plenty
to our confusion now, their cause somewhat
the Gadarene Revenge whereby one sow
may farrow twice in any year, bearing
upwards of two dozen. A whole kennel
of wolves, those gluttonous runnagadoes,
will fasten upon a single free-ranging hog
and reduce it to ribs and trotters ere
a farmer may fire a salute in the direction
of their banquet. Yet so common be
trespasses of swine through our fences

that some such bestial constabulary
might be considered against them. Swine laws
we have in excess, to be sure, but try
reading one to an object of its institution.
You will hear such a retort of snuffling
and snout music as the pig roots and grubs
for mast or so despoils a clam bank that
the Narragansetts fear the beast will drive
them to starvation. Thus the nodding assent
among them that a stray hog is as free
to the hunter as a deer or bear, nor will these
Indians pay such fines as our courts levy
against them. Indeed some be so bold-faced
as to offer fresh cuts of English pork for sale
to Englishmen. Further, the swine now threaten
to replace shillings and pence, since in their
aftermath as salt pork they have become
acceptable in divers places as payment for taxes.
Ere the frequent incursions of hogs into our villages
from outlying woods and fields result in
the carrying off of children as they play at poppets,
I propose the banishment of all swine in our colony
to the islands offshore, where they cannot
fatten wolves, or cause our hoodwinkt neighbors
east and north and west to sharpen their designation
of us from Island of Error to Island of Ordure.

8. Of Rivers, Theologies, and Persons Infamous
Roger Williams, 1671

The Woonasquatucket, the Sakonnet, its rocks
a terror to hulls, the Taunton, Warren, Swansea
and Moshassuck—boundary waters all,
each involved in our discordances. With
Massachusetts grinding away on one side
and Connecticut on the other, poor Rhode Island
seemed a miserable grain of corn between.
I could say those rivers contribute to this

Narragansett Bay as the sects we admitted
flooded our colony. The Sakonnet might be
the Familists, who believed in direct
inspiration from the Holy Spirit, God's Law
written on Adam's heart when His breath
quickened the clay. How many days did I stumble
across the gadfly Samuel Gorton wandering
among the trees at Shawomet, conversing aloud
with the Creator? And let the Pawtuxet River—
where that two-legged beast Richard Chasmore
practiced his lust on a heifer, and William
Harris tried to work his land-lust—stand for
the Quakers, their reliance on a "Divine Light"
within. The Woonasquatucket we might say
represents the Anabaptists, or perhaps
the Antipedobaptists, or the Seventh-Day Baptists
or Six-Principle Baptists, for we welcomed
whatever Baptists arrived, one and all, even as
these rivers contribute to this bay. Grindletonians,
Ranters, Socinians, Antisabbatarians. With liberty
of conscience all might think as they would,
Anglicans, Jews, even Papists. And so
to Rhode Island and Providence Plantations
came some who held that the Lord was present in
hogs, dogs, and sheep, or that a harlot
was sanctified when she married a godly man.
Conjure any theological point and we housed
its espouser or defender, so long as he made no riot,
provoked no gusts, caused no false military
alarms, and took no part in plots and diggings,
as with Irish pirates or Dutch grave robbers.
Nor would we welcome persons infamous,
as William Baker, much given to consorting
among Mohegan squaws at Pequot,
nor various wandering self-made squires and "Sirs,"
as Capt. George Wright, who flew like a cowbird
from bed to bed across these colonies, Plymouth
to Newport to New Netherlands, where he continued

his ungodly sports, apparently with Dutch approval.
Nor the Widow Messenger's daughter,
Sarah Neale of Boston, great in the belly though unwed,
with a mouth abusive and unstoppable, who called
our town a cage of unclean birds, and yet
would live among us to spite our teeth. The rigider
colonies call us Rogues Island, the *latrina*
of New England, where everyone thinks otherwise
from everyone. Still, we agree upon freedom of thought
and the walling of civil government from church.
There is no lopping of ears or lives to enforce orthodoxy,
no witch-burning. We have drunk deeply from
the cup of great liberties, none deeper, but I tell you
the din and clash of opposing doctrines has
converted me to a Seeker, one who awaits the cure
of the Second Coming, and wishes some days I had never
sold my trading post at Cocumscussoc, that nest
down this bay in the Narragansett country where
no disturbing hand could reach me, whose name
when I say it to myself is as salutary as
two crows calling across its benign coves.

9. A Second Coming at Providence Plantation
Roger Williams, 1678

As I was weeding in my squash patch,
I heard the braying, as of an ass,
down at the nether end of Towne Street,
the first I have heard since England,
and I do love those raggedy-faced beasts.
A crowd down there was milling about
some distraction, which parting
revealed the poor, rough animal in fact,
and mounted thereon, a hairy personage
surrounded by a cohort of apparent itinerants,
apple women and broom men I saw
as they came on, strewing wayside flowers
since we have no palms, disciples for this

latest holy imbecile making a progress
through our plantation, or so I prayed
as I viewed from my patch
the wooden face he maintained,
believing it stood for godliness, perhaps,
this new Lord our God or King of the Jews
or Prophet to the Colonies, his followers
at least keeping in their clothes this time,
the little beast supporting him the sole
original detail in his party. Across the ocean
he'd have died in chains, his troop
flayed with the lash for blasphemy. But here,
since liberty of conscience is our byword,
I let the parade pass, being a man
stricken in years, poking with his hoe,
deaf to the latest bewildernessed
tub preacher or mumbo-jumbo man
going down the street of Providence,
Bedlam's first town. What use
to fall together by the ears with another
self-appointed King and Messiah
headed for a beheading elsewhere,
as so often proves the case? He was fare
for a sermon, as I noted, and would leave
his sorry followers at some crossroads,
waiting for the next pulpit juggler,
tailor-at-law, or doctor of tavern flummery.
I thought of that bird in our bosom,
and of those birds who appear at sea
as out of nowhere, and grab onto
the ship's least spar against a beating wind.

10. Canoeing with Master Williams

> *Our ancient and approved friend, Roger Williams*
> *—John Thornton*

The root of a nearby apple tree
was growing in his grave after two centuries,

some claim, its form a human skeleton's,
as though he were the saint of orchardists
or founder of some golden age, the kind of elevation
he abhorred, though he loved the yellow sweetings
William Blackstone grew, and ordered
apples by the bushel. In truth he was buried
in a garden "by Patience Ashton's grave,"
though we know the place of neither,
and not one sermon of his remains. So with
his letters. Some folded by a goodwife
for seed packets, or crumpled under firewood,
others gone seaward in the hurricane of 1815,
and still more doodled upon, or skidded
by a breeze working a trashpile down
a Providence street, 1833. Burnt, lost and stolen,
maybe even forged; shoved into sacks
in offices and archives. The Narragansetts,
whose tongue he spoke and codified in his
Key to the Language of America, torched his home
and papers. Sorefooted, crippled, in age he went
upon a stick. Next time you're passing, look for
a canoe hewn from a single chestnut's trunk
and slipping off among freighters and barges
putting in at Providence, more fleeting wish
than ever in these days of collapsed
industrial rainbows floating like newfangled
jellyfish about him, among the steel craft
blind to him because he heaps up nothing for
God Commerce. He is going to Cocumscussoc
one more time. It wouldn't harm you to dip a paddle
with him. Anon he may explain how we began
with Providence Plantation and came to Plunderdome,
hirelings and hatchplots fleeing down the granite steps,
fists full of their God Money. Nor will it hurt
to hear him praise the Father of Lights for the Sea Turn,
that south wind coming early with the sun and
strengthening from the southwest toward noon.
Nor to hear the splash of his anchor stamped with *Hope.*

V

A Mile Down the Road from Home

I've caught myself
whistling a bumpy version
of "Take the A Train," and only
because this catbird
in a beachplum thicket has
taken me up on it
or close enough, the bird
keeping a breath or two behind
as if trying to hear where
I'm taking him, then diving
back into his own songline,
improvising along his strung-out
warbles and gutturals, and now
a few kingfisher rattles
and perhaps a black-billed cuckoo
or something else he's brought
up the hemisphere for this
season of courtship, cackles
and chucks, even a treefrog's piping.
I can feel Darwin frowning over me
like a thunderhead. A little
shaky about messing around
in natural selection, I look
both ways, taking care the bird
and I are alone before I donate
a ragged thread from *Peter Grimes*
to this slate-colored, black-capped
male who has only
a rufous undertail for flash.

The Mice

This morning in the cold shed
I unlocked two from traps
with a trowel, freeing them for
the brushpile where overnight
something will recycle them.

They are whole in this weather,
self-contained, and their eyes
looked up—beady, yes, but
sincere about their inability
to comprehend why chewing holes
in my rubber waders is wrong.

Then I remembered when you
were little how I used to tell you
I drove them to the P&B bus stop
and bought them tickets.

Can you still see them as I do now,
Dead End Kids clambering up the steps
in their plaid caps and plus fours,
heading for the back window
where they'll wave until the bus
turns for the highway?

Oyster Money

Stabbed by the heron's shadow
as the bird planed above me on these flats,
I am back in Taylorville, 1958,
scratching the low-tide mud with Linc
and his father, the Kaiser. "No future
in oysters, boy." The old man's advising
one or both of us to stay in school
or else enlist in the Navy: "Three hots
and a cot from Uncle Sammy, finest kind,"
he says. "No future in oysters." This
from a childhood of them nightly
staring back from his plate, Black Friday
to Pearl Harbor, and a lifetime
of digging, bagging, hauling, shucking
and selling, but not eating any more ever,
not on a half-shell or stewed, fried
and damn sure not Rockefellered.
When Linc and I cut out to deliver
to restaurants over on 6A and 28,
the old woodie's riding low with bushels
and so rusty that just the brine smell
could cause it to pass over into dust
after years of wet burlap and waiting
by salt water. On 6A the tourist cars
are wondering why a Bud can seems
to fall occasionally out of the sky.
When I take the wheel outside Lucky Jim's
and head for the Oceanside Inn, Linc draws
his guitar from behind the seat
and picks off "Under the Double Eagle"
and "Back Street Affair," and worries out loud
between tunes that we won't get home
in time to distract his father. "That man
can be some foolish with a dollar,
particularly a roll of oyster money
that could choke a horse." Which doesn't

prevent us from tilting another one
or two at a couple of taps where they find
our folded floppy hipboots colorful. We take
the side roads home, avoiding the cops
of three towns, and are too late. Because now
Kaiser's got friends, plus a Mr. Kenneth straw hat
with butterflies and little Bud cans on it,
and a yellow shirt plastered with Diamond Head
and upside-down palm trees, and not just
any friends but Boggsy, Billy Morna,
Captain Teabag, a gallery of harborside
slouches leaning on Jazz Garters' DeSoto,
its red and black matching their Carling cans.
The look on Linc's face is conveying
another winter under tarpaper. Kaiser
can't look at his boy. I can see he knows
what kind of friends he has, but he's
seeing the state road, too, empty ten months
of the year, and closing time,
and walking home from Mahar's in the rain.

Corps of Discovery
1803–1806

Framed in gilt in this oilman's Museum
of the West, they stand like spearbearers
in an opera staged for an insurance
company's calendar, not in rotting elkskins
at Cape Disappointment in a gray
Pacific rain. Cruzatte was a one-eyed fiddler.
Frequently drunk and disorderly,
John Collins was a *black gard,* as Capt. Clark
spelled it, and stole a farmer's pig.
For tapping the Corps' grog while on
guard duty, Collins was court-martialed
along with Hall. Werner was AWOL
in St. Charles, Missouri, and they
hadn't left the River Dubois
base camp yet. Bemused, Clark wondered
why Howard never drank water.

Near present-day Sioux City, Sgt. Floyd
died of a ruptured appendix. Catch
them before their moment
flashes like snowmelt and is gone.
Salt mountains, blue-eyed tribes
speaking Welsh, woolly mammoths
they'd heard about, and the grizzly,
cousin of the black bear and brown,
but not this wounded, tusked
embodiment of berserk they were entering
the thicket of broadleafed willow after,
this problem no high-minded thought
could neutralize as the breeze
abetted a rush of adrenalin.

Of Robertson—if that was his name—
we know nothing, nor Thompson nor
Isaac White. La Liberté spoke some Oto

but, true to his name, deserted
on a government horse. His other name
may have been Joe Barter, or else
there were two Joe La Bartees.
What has a head like a dog's with the ears
cut off, a groundhog's body with a white
stripe from nose-tip to shoulderblades,
and burrows after prairie dogs? Braro
is one answer. Spuck, louservia, simlin,
cabri, and butterbox are a few other names
for things they took with them through
the prickly pears and into History.

As far as it was possible to go, they went.
Three years and they disperse into their own
myths and legends. Stories that named
Stinking Bird River, Bad Place, and
Thigh-snagged Creek went with them. Colter
would return a mountain man with tales
of geysers and hot springs, and be
ridiculed for "Colter's Hell." Running naked,
he'd elude the Blackfeet who killed Potts,
and be hallowed for "Colter's Run."

Drouillard fell to the Blackfeet, Collins to
the Arikaras, the tribe that caused Shannon
to lose his leg before he went on to study law
and become a senator. Whitehouse deserted
the Army in 1817. Streams they named
are submerged in public drinking water,
places they camped, cursing the musquetors,
are bridge abutments on the Interstates.
Out hunting in a brake on the return
down the Missouri, Cruzatte the one-eyed fiddler
by mistake shot Capt. Lewis in the haunches.
Lewis died by his own hand at Grinder's Stand
on the Natchez Trace, October 17, 1809.

After twenty years, Clark's list of the 18 dead
or killed included Sgt. Patrick Gass,
who in fact lost an eye in the War of 1812,
married at 60, and lived to be 99. Done in oils
on a bluff above the Missouri or Rochejhone
or Snake or Columbia, anonymous in buckskins,
unencumbered by lead cans of portable soup,
surveyor's chains and carrots of tobacco,
or medals embossed with handshakes
and peace pipes, cleaned up for their formal
presentation to America, they seem iconic,
not men but heroes. Not one looks to be thinking,
"Experience is Wisdom." Under a sky still clear
of our haze of plenitude, they lean on
their Kentucky long rifles, backgrounding
Lewis who is pointing out to Clark
the direction of Manifest Destiny.

Hard Evidence

The silence after snow: all night its fall
of soft stars, cog-wheels and compass roses,
its random heaping of baroque medallions

has created air pockets that muffle sound,
and I see that I don't own this land, am only paying
the taxes for these others, my signature

on the checks as meaningful to possession as
this itinerant leaf's scribbled autograph. Before dog,
before me, an early coyote passed with a hint

of the fastidious in its step, a hint of mind where
it went up one side of that white dune, then retreated
another way. There's something of meditation

in the casual goings of foxes and coyotes,
while these birdprints dart to a destination,
no sense of sidetracking or inquiry. Look here

where littlefoot is a tail dragger, always in a hurry
from under that half barrel of dormant herbs.
It's the point where two vectors meet, hard evidence,

that turns this wind to a blade against bone,
the place of skid and scuffle, the start of erasure
back through palimpsest to tabula rasa.

Letter from Cold Harbor

Winter solitude—
in a world of one color,
the sound of wind.
     —Basho

True, but your wind is rippling these floorboards
like piano keys. It's ripping that nuthatch
out the window into new fletching for its arrows.
Though it's morning, another midnight cloud
leans in from Stellwagen Bank and explodes
its piñata of ocean effect snow—the sea
at thirty-eight Fahrenheit is warmer than
your wind, so there's more in the offing,
and more of that wind stomping around
on the roof over our heads, plucking and tossing
the shingles into those white knolls and ravines
it carved out there. The shingles look like
sugar wafers in ice cream, but only when we're not
thinking straight. We need the high whine
of a Yamaha outboard to restore a hint of normalcy,
or the sudden slushy throat-clearing rumble of
a cold International marine engine turning over
down at the pier, where a gull's flying in place
and your wind's turning mean corners
on icebergs it's sculpting. How many haikus
can dance on the head of a dragger's winch, Basho?
To hell with elegance: we need your wind
to carry at least a hint of the low-tide mud
at Dummer's Cove. Squalor, the smell of bait-bucket
squid beginning to thaw. And lose the mysticism,
make room for rumor—they say the ocean's
broken a hundred-foot channel through the dunes
at South Island, that the rate of domestic
violence is going to be off the charts.

How Winter Left Town

It looked like a band of archangels
had started a walkout in the high-bush
blueberry and chokecherry tangles
edging the fire road, divesting their wings
and tossing them in where the sun
doesn't touch down before the end of March,
and a few days later, at the base
of the high pines over there, I thought
I saw a line of off-white laundry
felled by the wind—the fool-me-twice
shape-shifting of the snow, its color
ascended into a full Worm Moon
later to be adored by thumb-sized frogs,
and the body of snow misted into air
to fall back elsewhere as rain,
and still more to fly up over marsh grass
in the grayed-out form of a northern harrier—
until, back down on earth and April
come to light, Thane Gould filled my tank
at Moxie's Sunoco, the only old snow
a sad rag hanging from his coveralls.

An Intermission

After the last snows and the first
April chive-bursts, two came in
off the flyway, not flying
but coasting, humped to catch the air,
their wings on the long glide
without a single beat. White as if
a breeze were buffing fresh snowbanks,
their wing-sound was like wind
over snow—two tundra swans
by their black bills, not the decorative
imports children toss old bread at
on public water, but long as a man
and spanned wide as an eagle. *Cygnus
columbianus,* named for the river
Lewis and Clark found them on,
they had come all the way from
Currituck Sound or the Chesapeake,
aimed for the high Arctic
nesting grounds. Like gods out of
their element, they floated past me
above the pond and on down
the riverine marshes, pagan, twinned,
impersonal in their cold sublimity,
blind to my witness, their necks
outsnaking, intent on a brief rest
somewhere on our little river.

Stations

History's braided with memory here at roadside:
it has all been provender and materia medica,
and may be again, the rose hips' dispensary,
cattails my daughter stirred to pancake batter,
those fiddleheads we clip for the frying pan,

even the purple-black fruiting clusters of pokeweed
that seem to wait for the passenger pigeon's return.

⟅∾

Since the road is like a Möbius strip looping river and marsh,
we can start anywhere: with sheep sorrel, maroon
against a wall of phragmites,

                                      back of the hudsonia
Aunt Margaret in her straw hat and Peck & Peck
linen coat used to shovel into the trunk
of one old Ford or another,

                                 or else we can begin with
the roadside eruptions of wild beachplum in May,
snowbanks the sun exempts.

⟅∾

Just around that bend, Phil Ryder's apple trees
look assembled of worn-out hipbones
and warbler loopholes not long for this world,

though there are whole June days
when I swear I could place two opposing parties
where a breeze off the pond startles their blossoms
and negotiate a lasting peace.

⟅∾

Here's cow vetch purple and ferny in the grass,
and wild asparagus tall as a man one day,
barely there the day before,

then a place I wouldn't stand on Midsummer's Eve,
here by the elderberries, though their midnight-blue fruits
did yeoman's service
                            in Joe Fugiggy's wine. Nor
would I gather spores of those bracken ferns that evening,
since to vanish at the moment of St. John's birth
is no parlor trick.

    ∾

One morning I found the anti-poet Dungallon
in a drunken snooze down there in that thicket of honeysuckle
and rosa rugosa, even for him a bower of bliss.

    ∾

Here's mallow leaves the Greeks and Egyptians ate,
foxgrape that lives as long as that mossbacked
snapping turtle that floats like its own islet in the river,

and red highbush sparkleberries where the mockingbird
holds out all winter without a sound, concerned
but unafraid when I whistle a private tune a few feet away,
hoping to get it back from her next summer.

    ∾

Old world escapees, indentures, daisies or day's eyes,
"wound-wort," in white, flat clusters, now called yarrow,
and "the poor man's weathergrass,"
                            scarlet pimpernel
close to the asphalt, shutting its flowers before storms,

dusty miller, named like a shortstop,
Johnny-jump-up and the soapwort bouncing Bet,
its leaves useful in a goodwife's laundries,
and celandine's yellow dye on hands collecting
the plant, stowaways all,

colonists of this seed hoard and pollen stash
a buzzard revolves above and moves on.